MW01062084

Symbols
&
Their
Meaning

Symbols & Their Meaning

Rudolph F. Norden

CPH™

SAINT LOUIS

Biblical references, unless otherwise indicated, are from the Revised Standard Version of the Bible, copyrighted 1946, 1952 © 1971, 1973. Used by permission.

Scripture quotations marked (NIV) are from The Holy Bible: NEW INTERNATIONAL VERSION, © 1978 by the International Bible Society. Used by permission of Zondervan Bible Publishers.

Copyright © 1985 by Concordia Publishing House,
3558 South Jefferson Ave., St. Louis, MO 63118-3968.
Manufactured in the United States of America.

Library of Congress Cataloging in Publication Data

Norden, Rudolph F.
    Symbols and their meaning.

    1. Christian art and symbolism—Meditations.   I. Title
BV150.N67   1985   246'.55   84-15591
ISBN 0-570-03949-5

7 8 9 10 11 12 13 14 15 16   03 02 01 00 99 98 97 96 95 94

To my sons
    Frederic,
    Ronald,
    and Martin

Contents

Preface

Symbols pervade our everyday life. The dollar bill, for example, shows not only the likeness of George Washington but also , on the other side, a pyramid with an eye in its detached tip, and this is balanced out with an eagle holding a branch in one claw and a cluster of arrows in the other.

Many companies, especially those of long standing, are recognized by identifying shields or other insignia. As you travel along a highway, you are guided by various signs to aid you in driving safely. Not only the shapes but also the colors of traffic signs have meaning. These fulfill their purpose if you can only catch them at a glance and know their significance. So it is also with commercial establishments along the way, such as service stations. They identify themselves by symbols such as the torch, the shell, the flying red horse. People who can't read words—and we are told that millions of Americans are illiterate—are helped by these visual aids.

In the readings that follow we examine symbols that likewise are forms of visual shorthand. They are of ancient origin. Early Christian burial places, such as the catacombs of the Basilica of St. Sebastian at Rome, show many symbols as scrawled graffiti: cross, fish, triangle in a circle, shepherd, dove, ship, and many more.

Christian symbols continue to have their place in the church life of today. Teachings or concepts that ordinarily would require many words to explain can be briefly projected as symbols. The knowledgeable viewer can grasp the idea at a glance. "Knowledgeable" should be stressed, for if viewers/worshipers are unfamiliar with the meaning, the emblem or sign conveys nothing. If not informed, they might even attribute mystic qualities to them as though they were ancient runes.

Christian symbols are excellent conversation openers; they can be useful in Christian witnessing, particularly if they prompt questions. If, for example, a caller or visitor asks what the symbol of the fish (*ichthys*, in Greek) on your front door means, you can explain that it is an acrostic that stands for "Jesus Christ, Son of God, Savior ." And having said that, you can follow through with a confession of personal faith and say that this Jesus "is my Lord." St. Peter tell us: "Always be prepared to give an answer to everyone who asks you to give the reason for the hope that you have" (1 Peter 3:15 NIV).

The cross, when worn as jewelry on a coat lapel or as part of a necklace, can likewise be a mark of identification. It says in effect—or so we may assume—that the wearer is making a statement of faith, as if to say: "In the cross of Christ I glory." It is by symbols such as the cross that Christians find one another while working, vacationing, or traveling together.

Interest in Christian symbolism has been greatly heightened in recent years through the making of banners, a favorite activity of many Christian individuals and groups. An insight into the message of symbols is essential both for the constructing and for the "reading" of these banner designs. The same is true when church women's groups sew paraments and vestments adorned with Christian monograms.

This book presents over 50 symbols, and it seeks to do this in a devotional setting. Not only are they explained as to their history and meaning, but they are also put into the context of the Christian faith. All in all, they are intended to present to the eye what the ear hears of the Word of God.

—Rudolph F. Norden

The Cross

The most widely recognized Christian symbol is undoubtedly the cross. Some 400 different forms have been created, many of them originating with heraldry—the cross was adapted to coats of arms, etc. Those signing up for the Crusades were said to "take the cross." Also today the cross occurs in secular or near-secular names and enterprises, such as the International Red Cross.

Some 50 types of crosses have been devised for church use. They occur not only as personal jewelry but also as art designs at church: on altar and pulpit hangings, in wood and stone, in stained-glass windows, atop steeples. The church building itself may be cruciform, that is, shaped like a cross, with the transept forming a right angle with the main part (nave) of the church.

Among the most common forms are the Latin cross, the Greek cross, and the Tau cross, as shown above. The Tau cross, minus the upper arm, is shaped like the Greek letter Tau, or the English T. It is sometimes called the Old Testament—or the prophetic or anticipatory—cross, because it is thought to resemble the pole on which Moses elevated the bronze serpent, to which Jesus referred: "As Moses lifted up the serpent in the wilderness, so must the Son of Man be lifted up, that whoever believes in Him may have eternal life" (John 3:14-15). Because it symbolizes the saving work of the prophesied Messiah, the Tau cross is particularly suitable for Advent.

The cross on which Jesus was crucified like a criminal was once an emblem of shame. But Christians regard it as a symbol of honor, saying with St. Paul that we should boast only "in the cross of our Lord Jesus Christ" (Galatians 6:14).

The Chi Rho Stands for Christ

From ancient times monograms have been used in Christendom. One of them is the Chi Rho, which stands for the first three letters of *Christos.* The Greek letter chi (ch) is written as the English capital letter X. The letter rho, also in the Russian alphabet, is like the English capital letter P. Russian writing, incidentally, is based on the Greek alphabet, due to early Eastern Church missionaries working among the Russians.

The Chi Rho occurs in various forms in the catacombs, the underground burial places where worship was often held out of sight of the pagans. Archaeologists have found it also on coins, lamps, pottery pieces, and as a grave inscription.

The Chi Rho sometimes appears together with the Alpha and Omega to affirm that Christ is the beginning and the end. The exalted Lord declares through St. John: "I am the Alpha and the Omega, the beginning and the end" (Revelation 21:6).

Fraternities and sororities on university campuses are not at all hesitant to display their Greek-letter names. Christians are also glad to let the world know about the brotherhood and sisterhood they have in Christ, whose monogram is Chi Rho. He is the Messiah, the Anointed One, whom they accept in their hearts and confess before the world as Lord and Savior.

The Chi Rho might well remind us of what Christ means to us in our daily lives. Here is a statement of faith written by St. Paul, in which all Christians can join: "It is no longer I who live, but Christ who lives in me; and the life I now live in the flesh I live by faith in the Son of God, who loved me and gave Himself for me" (Galatians 2:20).

IHC Stands for Jesus

A monogram that often adorns paraments, vestments, banners, and the like is the IHC. It stands for the first three letters of IHCOYC—or *Iesous,* if written in small letters—namely, Jesus. Another form of it is IHS, which is of later origin. The C comes closer to the way the Greek sigma (English S) was then written as a capital letter.

Other meanings have been read into this symbol, among them *Jesus Hominum Salvator,* which translates as "Jesus, Savior of Men," or *In Hoc Signo (Vinces).* The latter words, "In this sign you shall conquer," were supposedly spoken to Emperor Constantine to accompany the sign of the cross he saw in a vision during a battle which led to Christianity becoming the official religion of the Roman Empire. But it is better and more correct to take the IHC (or IHS) as simply denoting Jesus.

Sometimes the IHC is surrounded by the circle of eternity and set into the image of the sun. When so used, it reminds us the Messianic name given to our Lord in Malachi 4:2, the Sun of Righteousness. This symbol is especially appropriate for the Advent season.

The name of Jesus is precious to us. It bespeaks our salvation, according to what God said to Joseph in a dream: "You shall call His name Jesus, for He will save His people from their sins" (Matthew 1:21). That salvation completed, "God has highly exalted Him and bestowed on Him the name which is above every name, that at the name of Jesus every knee should bow, in heaven and on earth and under the earth, and every tongue confess that Jesus is Lord, to the glory of God the Father" (Philippians 2:9-11)

The Christmas Rose

The idea of a flower has long been identified with the Christ Child. A German Christmas carol opens with the line, *Es ist ein' Ros' entsprungen*— a Rose has sprung up. In its English translation, "Lo, How a Rose Is Growing," the reference to a flower is continued, for "a branch of Jesse's race" is said to "bear one perfect flower," and this is Jesus, descended from Jesse, David's father. Stanza four goes on: "This flower, whose fragrance tender With Sweetness fills the air, Dispels with glorious splendor The darkness everywhere."

Another source of the Christmas Rose symbolism is the legend that Joseph of Arimathea, having introduced Christianity into England in A.D. 63, planted a tree from which sprang a later tree at Glastonbury, England, which bursts forth with blossoms every Christmas Day.

In our time it is the poinsettia, introduced from Mexico and South America, that has taken over as the Christmas flower.

The Christmas Rose is an appropriate symbol of the Nativity of our Lord, not only because it blends in with the picture of Christ as the Branch (Zechariah 3:8, "Behold, I will bring My Servant the Branch") and Sprout (Isaiah 11:1, "There shall come forth a Shoot from the stump of Jesse") but also because of the declaration in the Song of Solomon (2:1 KJV): "I am the Rose of Sharon," which many Bible scholars attribute to the coming Messiah.

Christ, our Christmas Rose, is unique in His beauty: "Fair are the meadows, Fair are the woodlands, Robed in flowers of blooming spring; Jesus is fairer, Jesus is purer, He makes our sorrowing spirit sing."

The Star

Stars figured prominently in the lives of the ancients. The astrologists developed a pseudo-science, combined with religious beliefs, which dealt with the assumed influence of the stars on human affairs and with the foretelling of events on earth by their position in the heavens. To this day stars are used as symbols. The policeman's star is his badge of authority. Persons of brilliant qualities in drama or sport are called stars.

Stars are in evidence in our churches and homes—the five-pointed stars during the Advent-Christmas-Epiphany season. The significance we attach to them comes from the Bible. In the Old Testament the coming Savior is referred to under the figure of a star. Instead of cursing the children of Israel, Balaam blessed them in this prophecy: "A star shall come forth out of Jacob, and a Scepter shall rise out of Israel" (Numbers 24:17).

The festival of Epiphany marks the Christmas of the Gentiles. In the New Testament account of the coming of the Wise Men to worship Christ a star plays a prominent part, for it was seen by them in the East and it led them from Jerusalem to Bethlehem.

Stars—the real ones in the sky and the representations we make of them—are meaningful to Christians. They remind us of the Creator and His marvelous works. The psalmist calls the moon and the stars the handiwork of God's fingers. Even more, the star of this festival season points to the salvation performed by our blessed Savior, who through St. John tells us: "I am the Root and the Offspring of David, the bright Morning Star" (Revelation 22:16). May that Star always shine in our hearts!

The Shell
Signifies Baptism

Everyday life is full of symbols. Customers recognize products by their emblems, trademarks, labels. Motorists are aware of traffic signs and what they mean. Filling stations hang out their shields, and on them are such symbols as torch, star, and shell.

Symbols, long used in the Christian church, call attention to Biblical truths, particularly to events in the life and ministry of Jesus Christ. The shell with several drops of water dripping from it symbolizes both Jesus' baptism and ours.

No one was present with a camera to photograph Jesus' baptism. We don't know precisely how John the Baptist performed it—whether he used a shell, and the like. The evangelists Matthew, Mark, and Luke record these four events: (1) Jesus was baptized by John in the river Jordan; (2) He immediately came up from the water after He had been baptized; (3) He prayed; and (4) The Holy Spirit descended on Him like a dove, and the Father spoke from heaven: "This is My beloved Son, with whom I am well pleased."

Nothing is said in the text about a shell, but ancient pictures show John pouring water from a shell upon Jesus' head as He stands knee-deep in the water. The artists believed that the baptism of Jesus was performed in this manner. In some churches today baptisms are performed by pouring water from a shell. It reminds us that Jesus, the sinless Son of God, submitted to a sinner's baptism that He might "fulfill all righteousness" as Substitute, Savior, and Servant in our behalf. It should also remind us of our baptism, in which the Triune God made an eternal convenant of grace with each of us.

The Gospel for the World

The Christ born in Bethlehem of Judea and eventually crucified outside the city walls of Jerusalem is the world's Savior. The adoration of the Wise Men as representatives of the Gentile world underscores this truth. Some 700 years before the birth of the Messiah the prophet had said: "A multitude of camels shall cover you, the young camels of Midian and Ephah; all those from Sheba shall come. They shall bring gold and frankincense, and shall proclaim the praise of the Lord" (Isaiah 60:6).

Christianity is not a tribal religion. The blessings of the cross as announced in the Gospel are for people of all countries and cultures—in the words of St. Paul, for "Greek and Jew, circumcised and uncircumcised, barbarian, Scythian, slave, free man" (Colossians 3:11). The cross atop an orb signifies that the benefits of Christ's triumph over sin and death are to accrue to the peoples of the whole world.

As the curtain rises on the New Testament scene, we hear John the Baptist proclaiming as he points to Jesus: "Behold, the Lamb of God, who takes away the sin of the *world*"(John 1:29). Our Lord Himself testified that "God so loved the *world* that He gave His only Son" (John 3:16). Since His redeeming merit was gained for all, it is vital that the good news of it be made known to all. Hence the risen Savior's directive: "Go into all the *world* and preach the Gospel to the whole creation" (Mark 16:15).

The cross over the world—not the crescent, not the hammer and sickle—bespeaks Christ's lordship over the world by virtue of His atoning sacrifice and His resurrection. It remains for us to carry out His mission to all the world.

The Sword of the Spirit

Jan. 25 is the day the Christian church sets aside for the commemoration of the Conversion of St. Paul. The conversion of Saul the Pharisee was a most significant event. It meant that he who had availed himself of real swords as he breathed "threats and murder against the disciples of the Lord" – and who, in the words of Ananias to the Lord, had authority "to bind all who call upon Thy name" – was directly called by Christ to wield the spiritual sword of the Gospel as he carried His name "before the Gentiles and kings and the sons of Israel."

From that time on St. Paul worked zealously for his Lord, surrendering all of life's amenities that he might proclaim the Gospel, indeed not with physical might or power but by the Spirit. Hence the symbol for this apostle is a shield showing an open Bible on which the words *Spiritus Gladius* are written. These Latin words are "translated" by the sword behind the Bible, thus identifying the term as "the Sword of the Spirit."

St. Paul himself interprets this symbol for us in his words to the Ephesians (6:17): "Take the helmet of salvation, and the sword of the Spirit, which is the Word of God." The Epistle to the Hebrews (4:12) says of both Law and Gospel: "The Word of God is living and active, sharper than any two-edged sword, piercing to the division of soul and spirit, of joints and marrow, and discerning the thoughts and intention of the heart."

St. Paul accomplished much with the sword of the Spirit – with the preaching of the Word of God. The *Spiritus Gladius* is still the means for bringing sinners to saving faith in Jesus Christ.

Ichthys: the Creed in Brief

The fish, *ichthys* in Greek, is the symbol for the Savior Jesus Christ. It was so used already in the first century, not primarily because fish played a part in Jesus' life or because He appointed His apostles to be spiritual fishermen using the net of the Gospel, but because *ichthys* could be used as a rebus from which one could derive a statement of faith. The word consists of these five letters of the Greek alphabet: i-ch-th-y-s. When these five letters are regarded as initials for five words, we obtain this Christian declaration: *Iesous Christos Theou Yios Soter.* These words say: Jesus Christ, God's Son, Savior.

Very likely the *ichthys* symbol was used as a sign by which early Christians found and identified one another, especially in times of persecution. When scrawled on a wall or on the ground in the marketplace or near a fountain where people congregated, it let wandering Christians know that others of their faith had come to this community. A scene in a religious movie shows a man introducing himself to another by scratching the fish symbol into the sand before him.

The *ichthys* concept as explained is the Christian creed in brief: Jesus Christ is the Son of God and Savior of the world. St. John writes in his First Epistle: "We have seen and testify that the Father has sent His Son as the Savior of the world."

We can testify to our Christian faith today through the symbol of the *ichthys,* perhaps wearing it as a piece of jewelry or posting it as a door plate. When people ask what the picture of the fish means, we have a golden opportunity to explain who Jesus Christ is and what He means to us.

The Anchor of Hope

Old church cemeteries are good places for observing traditional symbols of the Christian faith, among them the anchor. From time immemorial this emblem has been seen on burial monuments. The anchor signifies the hope of Christians concerning the departed. St. Paul wrote to the Thessalonians about those who were asleep in Jesus, lest they "grieve as others do who have no hope."

The basis for associating the anchor with Christian hope is found in Hebrews 6:19-20: "We have this as a sure and steadfast anchor of the soul, a hope that enters into the inner shrine behind the curtain, where Jesus has gone as a forerunner on our behalf."

Christians have hope because Jesus has preceded them to the throne of the heavenly Father, having entered the holy of holies above after He had made atonement for sin and then risen from the dead. As the anchor holds the ship in place, so hope holds the believer to Christ. The hymn writer puts it like this: "My hope is built on nothing less Than Jesus' blood and righteousness."

The anchor as a token of hope pertains not only to the dead but to the living as well. The Christian's hope gives stability and support amid the winds of adversity. It distinguishes God's people from pagans, who have no hope and are without God in the world. When in life's troubles the adoption of Christians as God's sons and daughters seems unreal and without evidence, St. Paul bids them remember: "In this hope we were saved. Now hope that is seen is not hope. For who hopes for what he sees? But if we hope for what we do not see, we wait for it with patience" (Romans 8:24-25).

The Hand of God

There are familiar symbols for the Son of God (the Lamb, the Chi Rho monogram) and for the Holy Spirit, who is usually shown as the descending dove. But what is the symbol of God the Father? For many centuries of the Christian era no attempts were made to picture Him. After all, God had said to Moses: "You cannot see My face," and St. John declared in his gospel: "No one has ever seen God." At the baptism of Jesus the Holy Spirit was seen as a dove, but nothing was seen of the Father; only His voice was heard.

The closest attempt at portraying God the Father was to show the *Manus Dei,* the hand of God. The Bible speaks of the Creator's hand, whose fingers made the heavens and the heavenly bodies, as Psalm 8 declares. Again: "His right hand and His holy arm have gotten Him victory" (Psalm 98:1).

The hand of God is shown in Christian art in several positions. Sometimes it is the hand raised in blessing, with the thumb and first fingers extended, and the third and fourth fingers closed. The open hand of God, extended downward from a cloud, represents not so much God's power (as in Psalm 98) but His generosity in giving us all we need. It is a visual representation of Psalm 145:16: "Thou openest Thy hand, Thou satisfiest the desire of every living thing."

The hand of God shown above is surrounded by a cruciform nimbus, denoting not only the Father's holiness but also His great love in giving us His Son and sending Him to the cross for our salvation. The symbol of the hand of God reminds us that the heavenly Father's hand reaches out into our lives. It guides us, guards us, blesses us, and supplies all our needs.

The All-Seeing Eye of God

At the end of World War I a pastor asked a returning soldier how he had managed to avoid the many temptations of army life. The young man replied, "I remembered the Bible verse, 'Thou God seest me.' "

To Christians the knowledge that they live, move, and have their being under the all-seeing, all-knowing God is more than a deterrent from sin; it is a comfort to know that God's eye, as a popular song has it, is not only "on the sparrow" but also on His people, guiding and guarding them.

Someone has called the All-Seeing Eye "a rather disquieting symbol." The author goes on to say that in many ancient English churches, with their high pulpits and three-hour sermons, the Eye was much in evidence, as though to keep the worshipers from falling asleep. God's All-Seeing Eye, usually without the equilateral triangle of the Trinity surrounding it, has become an emblem of a well-known secret society.

The all-seeing eye and all-knowing mind of God survey all creation while we work or worship, wake or sleep. He beholds and holds the whole world in His hand – the sun and moon, the wind and rain, and also the "tiny little baby." His is not an evil eye, not an eye that sees only evil. It is benign, as the psalmist declares: "The Lord looks down from heaven upon the children of men, to see if there are any that act wisely, that seek after God"(Ps. 14:2). God wants to bless all the people that He has made and that His Son has redeemed. He wants to lead them closer to Him, their heavenly Father, through the Gospel proclaiming the salvation in Christ.

For Christians there is assurance, not threat, in the All-Seeing Eye.

The Pelican-in-Her-Piety

People may wonder what the image of a certain bird is doing in church. A white dove? Yes. A sparrow, perhaps, because Jesus spoke of one. But a pelican? The pelican is mentioned in the Bible, but not in a flattering way. It is listed among unclean birds, not to be eaten.

However, among medieval naturalists the pelican had a good reputation. It was believed that in a famine the mother bird plucks open her breast and, at the sacrifice of her own life, feeds the young with her blood. The legend may have started in *Physiologus,* a fanciful book on birds and animals written from a viewpoint of piety.

The Pelican-in-Her-Piety, as this scene is called, has been pictured in historic churches built in the Middle Ages. It can be seen on the exterior or interior of churches in Germany, France, and England, also on the dossal canopy in the Chapel of the Intercession in New York.

In a Eucharistic hymn Thomas Aquinas, a 13th-century theologian, refers to Christ's forgiving, life-giving blood after the manner of the "loving pelican." And that is the point that the Pelican-in-Her-Piety image wishes to make: She is a type of the self-giving Savior, who gave up His lifeblood so that sinners might live. The truth underscored by this symbol is that of the Atonement. In the Book of Revelation, for example, tribute is given to Christ in these words (5:9): "Thou wast slain and by Thy blood didst ransom men for God from every tribe and tongue and people and nation." In the same book, this (1:5-6): "To Him who loves us and has freed us from our sins by His blood and made us a kingdom, priests to His God and Father, to Him be glory and dominion forever and ever."

The Tri-Radiant Nimbus

In Christian art a device is used to identify someone as holy—an angel, an apostle, or Christ Himself. It is the nimbus, popularly called halo. If the light surrounds the entire figure, the device is called an aureole. Combining the nimbus with the aureole creates a flood of light to envelop the entire person.

Such glory emanated from Jesus when He was transfigured on a mountaintop. The sacred accounts in the gospels according to Matthew, Mark, and Luke stress the radiance suffusing Christ's face and figure: "His face shone like the sun, and His garments became white as light" (Matthew 17:2); "His garments became glistening, intensely white, as no fuller on earth could bleach them" (Mark 9:3); "The appearance of His countenance was altered, and His raiment became dazzling white" (Luke 9:29).

The kind of nimbus that appropriately adorns the head of the transfigured Savior is called tri-radiant; the rays go out in three directions to form a cross. Our Lord was indeed very close to the cross when He was transfigured. We follow the right order when we observe His transfiguration on the Sunday before Lent. Jesus revealed His glory before descending into the night of death.

St. Peter had confessed: "You are the Christ, the Son of the living God." Six days later the truth of Peter's confession concerning Christ's deity came to visible fulfillment on the Mount of Transfiguration, and it was also rendered audible by the words of the heavenly Father: "This is My beloved Son, with whom I am well pleased." After the night of His Passion the light would shine again from the risen and ascended Lord.

The Crown of Thorns and Nails

Perhaps the most widely known symbol of our Lord's Passion is the crown of thorns. It recalls the hymn lines from Bernard of Clairvaux's *Salve caput cruentatum:* "O sacred head, now wounded, With grief and shame weighed down, Now scornfully surrounded With thorns, your only crown."

The crown of thorns the soldiers plaited and then forcefully thrust on Christ's head was part of the mockery they devised. Before Pontius Pilate Jesus had borne witness to His divine kingship. The soldiers picked up on this affirmation in order to ridicule it. They put a scarlet robe on Him, a crown of thorns on His head, and a reed (or make-believe scepter) in His right hand. Then with the reed they beat the crown of thorns into His head, afflicting not only pain of body but also pain of soul and mind.

The penetrating thorns were in time followed by penetrating nails. It was to the cross that Jesus' hands and feet were nailed. After rising from the dead Jesus, appearing before the disciples, showed His credentials to unbelieving Thomas, inviting him to put his probing finger into the nail prints in His hands. "They have pierced My hands and feet," the Messiah had foretold in Psalm 22.

In Christian symbolism only three nails—another symbol of the Trinity—are traditionally shown, on the assumption that only one nail was used to affix Jesus' feet, one on another, to the cross. At all events, it is "By the cross, the nail, the thorn, Piercing spear, and torturing scorn" that Christ redeemed us. Our debt before God is canceled, for God set it aside, "nailing it to the cross" (Colossians 2:14).

Chalice and Passion Cross

One of the symbols of Christ's Passion is the combination chalice and Passion cross. The chalice or cup in this instance does not refer to the cup of Holy Communion but to the great agony Jesus had to endure, which Jesus referred to as a "cup."

The chalice, with the bitter content of suffering and dying that Jesus must drink, received mention prior to Gethsemane. When through their mother James and John asked for seats of honor and power in Christ's kingdom, the Master probed them: "Are you able to drink the cup that I am to drink?" (Matthew 20:22). The reference was clearly to His forthcoming Passion. The above outline of the chalice recalls this prayer of Jesus in Gethsemane: "Father, if Thou art willing, remove this cup from Me; nevertheless not My will, but Thine, be done."

The Passion cross is depicted as having pointed ends which like swords of sorrow and pain would penetrate the soul of Jesus during His Passion. Shadows of the cross had long ago fallen across the life and ministry of Jesus, beginning with the manger of infancy. The venerable Simeon in the temple had foretold that Christ would be rejected and that a sword would pierce His mother's soul.

Knowing that He must bear His own cross to Calvary, our Lord long before bade His followers to deny themselves, take up their cross, and follow Him. For many of His disciples through the centuries that cross has been like Jesus' Passion cross—tipped with sharp edges.

The chalice and cross also bring us blessings: forgiveness of sins, peace with God, eternal life. Because Jesus drained the cup of suffering and bore the cross, our "cup overflows" (Psalm 23:5) and our crosses are made light.

The Crowing Cock

One of the symbols of Christ's Passion is the crowing cock. It has been seen inside of churches and on top of church steeples. During the time of Jesus' trial before the Sanhedrin, Peter was warming himself at a fire in the court of the high priest's palace. There he denied knowing or being associated with his Lord. The crowing cock recalls that event.

To warn this apostle of what lay ahead, Jesus had said to him on Maundy Thursday evening: "This very night, before the cock crows, you will deny Me three times." "Cock-crowing" was the term given to the third watch or division of the night. The evangelist Mark reports that after Peter's third denial "immediately the cock crowed a second time." It was early morning on Good Friday.

The crowing cock has found his way into many carvings and paintings, as if to help Christians remember that not only Peter but all of us are at times tempted to deny our Lord. That is the message of the cock perched on top of the great clock of the Strasbourg cathedral. Whenever the figure of Peter appears moving among the apostles, the cock crows.

The cock calls us to do the very reverse of what Peter did, namely to confess Christ. Our Savior has said: "Everyone who acknowledges Me before men, I also will acknowledge before My Father who is in heaven" (Matthew 10:32). Again He tells us: "Watch therefore—for you do not know when the master of the house will come, in the evening, or at midnight, or at cockcrow, or in the morning" (Mark 13:35). Watchfulness and readiness to confess are marks of an alert faith.

"If you confess with your lips that Jesus is Lord and believe in your heart that God raised Him from the dead, you will be saved" (Romans 10:9).

The Wounded Lamb

Of the many symbols for Lent, that of the Wounded Lamb is perhaps the most poignant. It brings home the point: "Without the shedding of blood there is no forgiveness of sins" (Hebrews 9:22).

In both Old and New Testaments the Messiah is compared to a lamb. Isaiah speaks of God's Suffering Servant as "a lamb that is led to the slaughter." John the Baptist exclaimed: "Behold, the Lamb of God, who takes away the sin of the world!"

In Christian art and architecture the Lamb is shown in at least three postures. Sometimes the Lamb is depicted as lying on the Book of Seven Seals, the theme being taken from the Book of Revelation (5:12): "Worthy is the lamb who was slain, to receive power and wealth and wisdom and might and honor and glory and blessing!" As the divine Judge Christ has the right to reveal what God has planned for the world.

Then we see the Lamb carrying the banner of victory in token of Christ's resurrection. The motif of the triumphant Lamb is of ancient origin and is often seen in Rome's catacombs.

In its third role the Lamb is depicted as wounded. The nimbus about its head is in designation of Jesus as the true Son of God. It holds not the banner of victory but a staff in the form of a cross, reminding us of the bitter agony preceding Christ's triumph. From the mortal wound flows blood into a cup, or chalice, to symbolize the shedding of Christ's blood in atonement for the sins of the whole world.

St. Peter puts the shedding of Christ's blood in right perspective when he writes: "You were ransomed . . . with the precious blood of Christ, like that of a lamb without blemish or spot" (1 Peter 1:18-19). The cost was great, but our salvation is assured.

The INRI Monogram

A common symbol of the Passion is the INRI. If this monogram is affixed to the altar crucifix, worshipers see it throughout the church year.

INRI is shorthand. It stands for the Latin *Iesus Nazarenus Rex Iudaeorum*—"Jesus of Nazareth, the King of the Jews." Pilate ordered the superscription of the cross to be written in three languages: Latin, Greek, and Hebrew. Consequently Christian symbolism sometimes shows this inscription in the three languages. At times the INRI letters are written on a scroll attached to the top of the cross.

In John's gospel (19:19-20) we read: "Pilate also wrote a title and put it on the cross; it read, 'Jesus of Nazareth, the King of the Jews.' Many of the Jews [other people, too] read this title, for the place where Jesus was crucified was near the city." It may also have been near a public road.

It has been pointed out that people to be executed carried with them a white board inscribed with the accusation. For Jesus the charge was His affirmation of kingship. On arrival at the scene of crucifixion this board, or poster, was nailed to the head of the cross. As for the three languages, Latin was for the Romans, Greek for foreigners and travelers, and Hebrew (perhaps Aramaic) for the local people.

It seems that Pilate wished to taunt the local leaders by posting this superscription. At least, the leaders were quick to voice their objection, wanting the Roman governor to revise the charge from a statement of fact to a claim: "This man *said*, I am King of the Jews.'" But Pilate would not budge.

Jesus Christ, also in His deepest degradation, is Lord of lords and King of kings. All glory be to Him!

Palms, Signs of Victory

The branches of palm trees symbolize Jesus' triumphant entry into Jerusalem. We read in Matthew's gospel (21:8): "Most of the crowd spread their garments on the road, and others cut branches from the trees and spread them on the road." The branches were plucked from palm trees in gardens and along the way, and they were plaited or twisted into a kind of matting or green welcome carpet.

History tells us that Xerxes, Alexander the Great, and other notables were greeted with tree branches and a generous outpouring of flowers. In Jesus' case, John's account (12:13) seems to imply that the people, as they moved along in the procession, would continue to cut and scatter the branches.

Palm trees are mentioned often in the Bible. They gave fruit (dates) and were incorporated as decorative designs in Solomon's temple. Their large, feathery leaves were regarded as tokens of victory and peace. Consequently we read in the Book of Revelation (7:9) "I looked, and behold, a great multitude . . . before the throne and before the Lamb, clothed in white robes, with palm branches in their hands."

Christ's followers have a share in His triumph over sin, death, and the devil. Catechumens who on Palm Sunday renew and confirm their baptismal vow with the Triune God do so not in reliance on their own strength but on Christ's victory. While every catechumen has an individual confirmation verse, here is one common to all: "Whatever is born of God overcomes the world; and this is the victory that overcomes the world, our faith. Who is it that overcomes the world but he who believes that Jesus is the Son of God?" (1 John 5:4-5). Today we may carry palms in memory of our own confirmation.

Easter Lily: Picture of Eternal Life

With Christ's resurrection on Easter morn the Christian's faith is greatly quickened, for "Now, after gloom and sadness, Comes forth the glorious Sun," as Paul Gerhardt has taught us to sing. Following the cold, cheerless winter of our sins there now emerges the springtime of our salvation in the risen Savior.

Among the many symbols of Christ's resurrection, the Easter Lily is undoubtedly the favorite and most familiar. For this two reasons can be cited. First, the Easter Lily is readily available. It is a spring flower that blooms during the Easter season. Second, the Easter Lily is a flower of extraordinary beauty, its white color symbolizing purity.

Plants make excellent symbols of the resurrection, both Christ's and ours. The Savior said: "Unless a grain of wheat falls into the earth and dies, it remains alone; but if it dies, it bears much fruit" (John 12:24). Christ's dead body lay buried in the earth, but on Easter morning He returned to life. Now He grants us the privilege of participating in the life He has resumed, not only in that we, in repentance and faith, daily rise to newness of life by virtue of our baptism, but in that we will on the Last Day rise to life in our glorified bodies. St. Paul wrote of the body: "It is sown in dishonor, it is raised in glory. It is sown in weakness, it is raised in power" (1 Corinthians 15:43)—and raised in purity, as we are reminded by the white Easter Lily.

We have this word from the apostle: "Christ . . . abolished death and brought life and immortality to light through the Gospel" (2 Timothy 1:10). This was done by Him who declares: "I am the Rose of Sharon, and the Lily of the valleys" (Song of Solomon 2:1 KJV).

The Peacock: Resurrection

The front of the altar in the church which this writer attends shows, among other designs, two peacocks facing each other as they drink from a water container that looks like a chalice. What do these exotic birds symbolize?

In a prescientific age myths sometimes got mixed in with facts. People then believed in non-existent creatures like the phoenix or griffin, or they associated all kinds of ideas with the unicorn (wild ox or rhinoceros) on land and the leviathan (crocodile or whale) in the water.

The peacock, unlike the phoenix, is a real fowl. It was known long ago. The Bible tells us that King Solomon imported "gold, silver, ivory, apes, and peacocks." Although real birds, peacocks became the subjects of two dubious beliefs: (1) that their flesh was incorruptible, and (2) that from year to year, as peacocks molted, the feathers would be replaced by even more brilliant ones.

The above may have been the reasons why early Christian artists and craftsmen used the peacock as a symbol of immortality and the resurrection, not only as far as Christ was concerned but also for those who believed in Him. We find the symbol so used in Byzantine art, as well as in many churches in England and on the Continent.

When peacocks are depicted as drinking from a vase or other vessel, they represent Christians partaking of the water of life, that is, of forgiveness of sins, life, and salvation, which Jesus imparts through the means of grace: Word and sacraments. It is only through the saving Gospel—as proclaimed verbally or as rendered visible in the sacraments—that faith is nourished and our grasp on eternal life is firmed up.

The Phoenix: Renewed Life

Cities destroyed by fire rise anew from the ashes. Plants that grow from bulbs die at the end of the season, but the next spring they are back. Psalm 103 speaks of the eagle renewing its youth. Renewals like this may have been in the minds of ancients as they made up stories about the wonder bird, the phoenix.

It was claimed that in the Arabian desert the phoenix, a bird supposedly resembling the eagle, built its nest of twigs and spices and lived in it for some 500 years. At the end of that period the sun's hot rays would set the nest afire and the phoenix, instead of smothering the flame, would fan it by flapping its wings, burning itself up in the fire. Then, in a renewed, refreshed body, it would rise from the ashes, rebuild its nest, and live on for another 500 years.

The phoenix, legendary though it was, caught the interest of people through the centuries. The coins of emperors in the East bore its image. Its likeness was seen on many ancient sarcophagi (stone coffins). In the Christian era it appeared as a church symbol, unmistakably as an emblem of immortality.

More specifically, the phoenix in Christian circles stood for bodily resurrection—first for the resurrection of Jesus Christ and then for that of the believers.

These were the first Christian truths St. Paul was taught after his conversion: "...that Christ died for our sins . . . that He was buried, that He was raised on the third day . . ." (1 Corinthians 15:4). From death—and from the grave, its chamber—Jesus rose to life again. From that event follows the fact of our resurrection on the Last Day and our return to life, eternal life.

Jesus, the Good Shepherd

Jesus is represented as the Good Shepherd in early Christian art—in the paintings of catacombs (Rome, Naples, Sardinia, Sicily) but not only there. As early as A.D. 210 Tertullian said he had seen the Good Shepherd symbol on chalices and lamps. On the rear wall above the baptismal font of a chapel built about A.D. 250 at Dura-Europos (in modern Syria) the Good Shepherd and His flock are depicted.

The earliest representations show a beardless youth, dressed in a tunic, carrying a lamb on his shoulders, in keeping with the saying of Jesus that the searching shepherd, having found the lost sheep, lays it on his shoulders and carries it home with rejoicing. The three-rayed nimbus identifies the shepherd as Jesus, the Son of God. He is shown as a sturdy youth, as one who, like young David, could protect his flock from wolves and other marauders.

Not only the equating of Jesus with the Good Shepherd—an identification Jesus Himself made—but also the picturing of church members as His sheep is a practice of ancient standing.

The Good Shepherd's insignia is sometimes shown as a cross-adorned banner attached to a shepherd's crook.

Jesus is still the Good Shepherd, attending to the needs of the flock for which He laid down His life and assumed it again. And we are still His sheep. Though we were straying like sheep, we have now been returned to the Shepherd and Guardian of our souls, as St. Peter assures us in the traditional epistle for Good Shepherd Sunday. We were rescued from straying and returned to His fellowship through Holy Baptism.

The Butterfly Depicts New Life

One of the most beautiful of all symbols of the resurrection and of life eternal is the butterfly. The life of a butterfly, brief as it is, consists of three distinguishable stages.

First, the butterfly is a crawling larva, or cater-pillar—no beauty there, since people consider it a worm. Second, the delicate creature goes into its chrysalis (cocoon) stage. It has withdrawn itself into a shell—sealed itself up in an envelope. Third, it breaks its silk overcoat and bursts out of its cocoon. It emerges as a mature butterfly, with a beautiful new body and brightly colored wings to match. The wings soon dry, and the butterfly soars heavenward.

It is easy to see how the three-stage life of a butterfly resembles the lowly life, the death and burial, and the glorious resurrection of Christ. Born in the likeness of human beings—in the form of a servant, in fact—our Lord "had no form or comeli-ness . . . no beauty that we should desire Him," as Isaiah wrote. Pilate's "Behold the Man!" implies a beaten figure whose broken, lifeless body was soon to be laid into a grave. In the tomb our Lord rested. But on the third day Jesus emerged alive with a glorious body, and in that body He ascended into heaven 40 days later.

Also those who belong to Christ pass through the three stages. By nature sinful, mortal persons, their condition in life is lowly. Death comes, and the lifeless body is buried in weakness. But on the Last Day, when Christ shall return in all His glory, Christians shall come forth with changed bodies modeled after Christ's glorious body. How wonderful the new life in Christ!

The Ascended Lord Is Crowned

Various symbols have been noted in ancient Christian sites to denote Christ's ascension, some of them combining it with the bodily assumptions of human beings: Elijah's ascent in a fiery chariot (seen on the tombs of martyrs), the translation of Enoch, and the last ascent of Moses into a mountain from which God took him to heaven.

Sometimes the quartrefoil (four-leaf flower), with the Messianic Rose imposed on it, betokens the Ascension, the four leaves referring to Christ's command to bring the Gospel to the four corners of the earth.

Perhaps the most appropriate symbol of the Ascension is the Crown and Scepter. It denotes Christ's kingly office, to the full exercise of which He returned with His ascent into heaven. Having begun the state of exaltation with His quickening in the grave, Jesus with His bodily return to God's right hand resumed His kingship over heaven and earth. Enthroned in heaven, He fills all things, ruling over angels and saints and also keeping the enemies of His church in check. There remains only this: "Then comes the end, when He delivers the kingdom to God the Father after destroying every rule and every authority and power" (1 Corinthians 15:24). On the Last Day the King will return to "wrap things up," as we say in everyday parlance.

What has been called our Lord's coronation hymn declares: "All hail the power of Jesus' name! Let angels prostrate fall; Bring forth the royal diadem And crown Him Lord of all."

Crowns await also those who persevere in the faith, remaining faithful to their heavenly King until death. He will grant them "the crown of life" (James 1:12).

The Bursting Pomegranate

What a difference there is between a fearfully destructive grenade (a French word, derived from the Latin *malum granatum*—an apple full of seed) and a nourishing, refreshing pomegranate. The first kills with its fragments, the second gives life.

The pomegranate is a fruit about the size of an orange. It is full of kernels contained in tasty red pulp, and its juice is like wine. It is mentioned in the Bible. A favorite fruit, it was used as a pillar decoration in Solomon's temple and as an ornament on the high priest's robe.

The bursting pomegranate has various meanings. It can designate the truth that Christ has burst forth from the grave on Easter morning. So Christians, too, will burst the bonds of death. With its rind opened, the pomegranate is shown to be full of good things to enjoy. That makes it a symbol not only of Christ's resurrection as an event but also of the blessings He imparts. The good news of Christ's return to life assures Christians of the certainty of forgiveness, peace with God, the hope of the life to come, and the resurrection of their own bodies on the Last Day. St. Paul speaks of all this at the beginning of his Letter to the Ephesians, saying that God "has blessed us in Christ with every spiritual blessing." In Christ God has lavished all His gifts on us.

The pomegranate, in view of the good things it produces in abundance, is symbolic also of the fertile power of God's Word and the riches of divine grace. Through Isaiah God declares that His Word shall "prosper in the thing for which I sent it" (55:11), and St. Paul teaches: "Where sin increased, grace abounded all the more" (Romans 5:20).

The Spirit of Pentecost

The most frequent representation of the Holy Spirit is the descending dove. It is also one of the earliest. It has been beautifully executed in Christian art. The best examples show the dove with the three-rayed nimbus to indicate that the Holy Spirit is the Third Person of the Trinity. The favorite place for this symbol to appear in early churches is the cover of the baptismal font.

The basis for picturing the Spirit as a dove is found in what the four evangelists report about the baptism of Jesus, namely, that the heavens were opened and that the Holy Spirit came upon Him in the form of a dove.

The association of the Holy Spirit with baptism rests also on Jesus' words to Nicodemus that all who would be in His kingdom must be born again of water and of the Spirit. Further, St. Paul refers to the sacrament in Titus 3:5, calling it "the washing of regeneration and renewal in the Holy Spirit."

In the account of the outpouring of the Spirit on Pentecost (Acts 2) no mention is made of a dove. The sound on that occasion was that of the mighty rushing wind, and the outward sight consisted of tongues of fire. The text goes on: "They were all filled with the Holy Spirit." From the Pentecost event came other symbols of the Holy Spirit, such as a flame of fire (or seven flames) and the seven burning lamps symbolizing the seven gifts of the Spirit.

Early Christian monuments for the dead show doves to declare the innocence of the departed, in remembrance of Jesus' words: "Be wise as serpents and innocent as doves" (Matthew 10:16). Innocence, too, is a fruit of the Spirit.

The Holy Trinity

Already in the first centuries false teachers, including Arius, attacked the doctrine of the Triune God. The Nicene Creed, as a confessional bulwark against Arianism and kindred heresies, declares Jesus Christ to be equal with the Father. The Athanasian Creed stresses with great clarity that the three Persons of the Godhead are equal: "In this Trinity none is before or after another; none is greater or less than another. But the whole three Persons are coeternal together and coequal, so that in all things . . . the Unity in Trinity and the Trinity in Unity is to be worshiped."

One of the oldest emblems of the Trinity is the equilateral triangle. The sides and angles are equal. Together they form but one figure. This symbol is a visual aid in support of the truth that the three distinct Persons: Father, Son, and Holy Spirit, are coequal. It shows further that the three Persons constitute a unity—one divine essence.

The triangle enclosed in a circle points not only to divine unity but also to divine eternity. As the three Persons are coequal in honor and power, so they are coeternal, not one before or after the other.

Any illustration of the Trinity, verbal or visual, is at best an approximation of the truth of God's being. We cannot grasp the nature of God with our minds. But we can accept in faith what God has revealed of Himself in His Word, and we can worship the Triune God with all our heart as we exclaim with St. Paul: "O the depth of the riches and wisdom and knowledge of God! How unsearchable are His judgments and how inscrutable His ways!" (Romans 11:33).

The Seven Gifts of the Spirit

The seven-branched candlestick in the temple was called the menorah. It burned uninterruptedly as worship was made to the continually present God. In the opening chapter of Revelation St. John speaks of the "seven golden lampstands."

Fire is associated with the Holy Spirit. On Pentecost Day the Spirit appeared as with fiery tongues, and Jesus referred to the baptism with the Holy Spirit and with fire. The seven flames of the candlestick were considered emblematic of the seven gifts of the Spirit. These are mentioned in the Bible. Isaiah writes (11:2): "The Spirit of the Lord shall rest upon Him, the Spirit of wisdom and understanding, the Spirit of counsel and might, the Spirit of knowledge and the fear of the Lord." The Book of Revelation (4:5) mentions the "seven torches of fire" that burn before God's throne. It speaks in the next chapter of these seven gifts given to the Lamb: power, wealth, wisdom, might, honor, glory, and blessing.

It is not only to Christ that the seven gifts of the Spirit were given. Believers, too, receive them. At confirmation this blessing is bestowed with the laying on of hands: "God, the Father of our Lord Jesus Christ, give you His Holy Spirit, the Spirit of wisdom and knowledge, of grace and prayer, of power and strength, of sanctification and the fear of God."

Sometimes spiritual gifts are given in floodtide, as in the apostolic age. They are called charismatic gifts, and the Holy Spirit distributes them as He wills, to whom He wills, and where and when He wills.

Basic for every Christian is the Holy Spirit's gift of faith in the Savior, Jesus Christ.

The Nine Fruits of the Spirit

In 1 Corinthians 12:4-11 St. Paul mentions nine charismatic gifts of the Spirit: utterance of wisdom, utterance of knowledge, heroic faith, gifts of healing, the working of miracles, prophecy, the ability to distinguish between spirits, various kinds of tongues, and the interpretation of tongues.

Perhaps by coincidence—if not due to some inward connection—there are also nine fruits of the Spirit, as enumerated in Galatians 5:22 by the same apostle: love, joy, peace, patience, kindness, goodness, faithfulness, gentleness, self-control. Together they form one cluster—the *fruit* of the Spirit. St. Paul plays them off against the aforementioned 15 "works of the flesh."

The nine charismatic gifts imply speaking and doing; the nine fruits bespeak Christian qualities, characteristics, and attitudes of the heart. Perhaps the connection between the two sets of nine is that the heart must be renewed before there can be God-pleasing words and works.

The nine fruits of the Spirit are represented by the nine-pointed star. In the tips of the star are these letters: C, G, P, L, B, B, F, M, and C. These stand for the Latin words for the virtues listed in Galatians 5:22, given in English above: *Caritas, Gaudium, Pax, Longanimitas, Benignitas, Bonitas, Fides, Mansuetudo,* and *Continentia.*

Although we are now in the nonfestival half of the church year and are without the faith-lifting experiences of the great festivals, it is always the right season for spiritual growth and for yielding the fruits that the Holy Spirit works in us through Word and sacraments.

Christ the Vine

A design lending itself well to embroidery work, wood and stone carvings, and stained-glass windows is the vine with its branches. The vine represents Christ, who tells us in John 15: "I am the vine, you are the branches." Grape growing was widely practiced in the Holy Land, especially in the hill country of Judah. In referring to Himself as the stem that sustains the branches, our Lord was using an illustration that was well understood.

The symbol of the vine is seen in many of the older country churches in England. In many instances the vine is carved into see-through rood screens between the chancel and the nave of the church. Examples of vine moldings exist also in the United States, in chapels, churches, and cathedrals.

Sometimes small shields on which the apostles' names and symbols are written are attached to the plant. The branches symbolize the church, which is Christ's body. The birds that are at times shown nesting in the branches represent the souls of believers.

Few symbols so effectively illustrate the close union of Christ with the members of His church as does the figure of the vine and branches. Jesus declares: "He who abides in Me, and I in him, he it is that bears much fruit." All who abide in Him, that is, who take His words to heart and do them, are blessed in having Christ abide in them and in having His strength made perfect in them so that they can bear fruit. As a branch or tendril thrives in its connection with the stem and root system, so Christians become fruitful in all good works as they remain in Christ through diligent use of prayer and the Word.

The Winged Man: Matthew

When sculptors, painters, or stained-glass designers had four spaces to fill in a church building, they usually used the symbols for the four evangelists: the winged man for Matthew, the winged lion for Mark, the winged ox for Luke, and the eagle for John.

Why the winged man for Matthew? In his gospel this evangelist stresses the human nature of Jesus Christ, the Son of God. The opening verse reads: "The book of the genealogy of Jesus Christ, the son of David, the son of Abraham." Matthew, writing from a Hebrew point of view, traces the lineage of Jesus to establish that He is truly a descendant of Hebrew forefathers.

The concept of a winged man seems to be based on a vision of the prophet Ezekiel in which he saw four winged creatures, each of which had the face of a man, a lion, an ox, and an eagle. In Christian art these four figures are shown with a nimbus to indicate that they are heavenly beings.

Matthew himself, prior to his call into the apostleship, was not a winged, or angelic, man. He had been a publican, a hated tax collector, in the service of either the Romans or their puppet, King Herod. We are not specifically told that he cheated, as Zacchaeus had done, but overcharging the taxpayers was pretty well built into the system of "farming out" to the highest bidders the business of collecting taxes. Matthew's name before he became a follower of Jesus was Levi. Many others who had a change of heart also changed their names.

We are thankful that Matthew wrote his gospel, particularly that he recorded these words of Jesus (20:28): "The Son of Man came not to be served but to serve, and to give His life as a ransom for many."

The Winged Lion: Mark

The four gospel writers, Matthew, Mark, Luke, and John, are shown in Christian art as these four winged beings, respectively: man, lion, ox, and eagle. This imagery seems to be based on a vision of four creatures described by Ezekiel in his opening chapter: "Each had the face of a man in front . . . the face of a lion on the right side . . . the face of an ox on the left side . . . the face of an eagle at the back." The same four creatures are mentioned in chapter 4 of the Book of Revelation.

The winged lion is the symbol of Mark. Why? Mark stresses the power and activity of Christ, emphasizing His strong deeds. Jesus is "the Lion of the tribe of Judah" (Revelation 5:5). This divine title denotes the divine nature and power of Christ. While Matthew stresses the human family tree of Jesus, Mark emphasizes the deity of our Savior, as becomes evident from the opening verse of his gospel: "The beginning of the Gospel of Jesus Christ, the Son of God." Christ, to whom Mark bears witness, is the King of kings, as the lion by reason of his strength is the king of beasts. By His power Jesus took up His life again on Easter morning, another reason why in early Christendom Jesus was regarded as a lion. We sing in an Easter hymn: "Lo, Judah's Lion wins the strife And conquers death to give us life. Hallelujah!"

Mark is closely associated with Peter, and we can see that impulsive disciple's personality coming through in Mark's vivid style of writing.

There is much our Lord has told through the evangelist Mark, including this: "Go into all the world and preach the Gospel to the whole creation."

The Winged Ox: Luke

From almost the beginning of the Christian era have the evangelists Matthew, Mark, Luke, and John been symbolized as a winged man, a winged lion, a winged ox, and an eagle.

The Book of Revelation tells us of a heavenly scene (4:6-7): "Round the throne, on each side of the throne, are four living creatures . . . the first . . . like a lion, the second . . . like an ox, the third . . . with the face of a man, and the fourth . . . like a flying eagle." Similar creatures are mentioned by Ezekiel.

In Christian art Matthew is designated as the winged man (he stressed the humanity of Jesus), and Mark as the winged lion because of his emphasis on Jesus' power and deity.

Why Luke as the winged ox? Oxen were sacrificial animals in Old Testament times. Luke, although of Gentile origin, was aware of the place of sacrifices among the Israelites. He opens his gospel with the story of Zechariah, a priest, performing a sacrifice at the time he was told that he would be the father of John the Baptist. He duly reports how Mary and Joseph brought a sacrifice after Jesus' birth, in keeping with the law of Moses. He pictures Jesus as the compassionate Servant of the Lord, as prophesied by Isaiah. Above all, Luke repeatedly emphasizes God's free forgiveness—a forgiveness made possible through Christ's sacrifice of Himself on the cross. For these reasons Luke is designated as the winged ox.

All of Scripture, of course, teaches Christ's atonement. The Epistle to the Hebrews brings out that the sacrifice brought by Jesus when He shed His blood was far superior to shedding "the blood of goats and bulls." Christ alone saves.

The Eagle: John

The Lord, says the psalmist (18:10), "came swiftly upon the wings of the wind." In response to all God's goodness, Christians seek to give wing to His Word. It is God's will that the Gospel move swiftly from place to place as though borne by winged messengers.

From time immemorial the four evangelists have been pictured as heralds with wings: Matthew as a winged man, Mark as a winged lion, Luke as a winged ox, and John as an eagle.

The Bible often refers to the wings of an eagle. It was considered to be the bird that could fly the highest. The evangelist John is rightly compared to an eagle, for, as someone has written, "from first to last his Gospel soars on eagles' wings to the very throne of Heaven." By the power of the Holy Spirit he rose to the highest level of contemplation as he recorded the eternal Word.

Further, in his gospel John stresses the divine nature of Christ in the most sublime terms. He begins his account: "In the beginning was the Word, and the Word was with God, and the Word was God." He makes clear that he is speaking of Jesus Christ, for he goes on: "The Word was made flesh and dwelt among us . . . full of grace and truth." John dwells on the exalted themes of our Lord's teaching—that God so loved the world as to send His only Son, that He and the Father are one, that to know Him and the Father is to have eternal life, that He would send the Spirit of Truth. Only John's gospel has Jesus' sublime High Priestly Prayer (chapter 17).

There is loftiness in John's gospel, and for that reason he is designated as the eagle that so often adorns pulpits and lecterns.

The Incense of Prayer

The incense burner typifies prayer. The rising smoke and sweet fumes suggest the rising of the Christian's prayer to God. The psalmist (141:2) asks God: "Let my prayer be counted as incense before Thee."

Implied in the above request is the hope that God will find our prayers acceptable, pleasing, and sweet-smelling. Incense burning was needed at the sacrificing of animals to take away the odor of burning carcasses. As God was pleased with sacrifices performed in faith, so He is pleased with prayers that ascend to Him from a pure and loving heart—the heart of a true believer in Christ.

Prayer is the Christian speaking with God in faith in Jesus Christ. It is "the soul's sincere desire, Unuttered or exprest." Various types of prayer are praise, thanksgiving, petition, supplication, and intercession. We pray privately or as a family group. We also pray in church as the larger family of God. Prayer is an important part of the liturgy. Prayer is a *sacrifice* in which *we give* our hearts to God, in distinction to a *sacrament* in which *God gives* us His grace.

We worship God as He wants us to when we pray with confidence and in Christ's name. The XP atop the symbol of the censer stands for *Christos,* for Him who reconciled us to God and by His death made us and our prayers acceptable to the heavenly Father.

Not only prayers but everything that Christians desire, think, speak, and do is like a sweet-smelling savor to God, thanks to Christ. Writes St. Paul: "Walk in love, as Christ loved us and gave Himself up for us, a fragrant offering and sacrifice to God" (Ephesians 5:2).

Christ, the Rock of Salvation

Many hymns refer to Christ as the Rock of salvation, the best known being Augustus M. Toplady's "Rock of Ages, Cleft for Me." There are others, known to us by familiar lines: "On Christ, the solid Rock, I stand; All other ground is sinking sand," or "Built on the Rock the church doth stand, Even when steeples are falling."

Christ is the Rock of salvation from several points of view. For one thing, He is the Source and Fountainhead of the water of life, as St. Paul writes: "They [the Israelites] drank from the supernatural Rock which followed them, and the Rock was Christ" (1 Corinthians 10:4).

The symbol of Christ the Rock suggests solidity and security, as expressed in Psalm 18:2, "The Lord is my Rock, and my Fortress, and my Deliverer." Again: "Let us make a joyful noise to the Rock of our salvation" (Psalm 95:1). The cross atop the rock recalls for Christians that Christ became the sure basis of their faith by dying on Calvary's cross for their sins and thus gaining their peace with God.

Christ is the Rock of salvation also from the viewpoint that His teachings are the truth, and all who believe in Him and obey Him have found a sure foundation for daily Christian living. Our Lord Himself compared such people to a man who built his house on a rock. That house, despite the inclement elements, did not fall "because it had been founded on the rock" (Matthew 7:25). The rock on which Christ builds His church is the word of the Gospel, as Peter confessed it in brief: "You are the Christ, the Son of the living God" (Matthew 16:16). God's Zion is secure, for it is founded on the Rock of Ages.

The Harp: Music and Worship

First, the harp is a symbol of musical talent such as David, "the sweet psalmist of Israel," possessed. While in the service of King Saul, David played the harp to dispel the king's dark moods. He used the harp, or lyre, to accompany the psalms he sang to the glory of God.

Second, the harp in a more general sense denotes joyful worship. The writer of Psalm 33 declares: "Praise the Lord with the lyre, make melody to Him with the harp of ten strings!" Psalm 150 mentions other instruments for praising God: trumpet, lute, timbrel, strings, pipe, and cymbals.

Third, the joy of worshiping God with the harp is a foretaste of our worship in heaven. St. John writes in the Book of Revelation (14:2-3) that the voice he heard from heaven "was like the sound of harpers playing on their harps, and they sing a new song before the throne." In another vision he sees the conquerors of the beast "standing beside the sea of glass with harps of God in their hands" (15:2). Such references to harps have led some people to think that all that the saints do in heaven is to play harps—an erroneous idea! It is doubtful whether those who on earth had calloused hands or who couldn't tell one note from another will be harpists in heaven. God has provided other things for them to do in order to occupy themselves creatively and to glorify Him.

Back on earth, the harp reminds us of the sweet harmony of music and how that kind of harmony should characterize our relationship to God and to one another in the unity of faith. The psalmist exclaims (133:1): "Behold, how good and pleasant it is when brothers [and sisters] dwell in unity!"

The Lamp of Knowledge

From ancient times lamps were lit to dispel *physical* darkness—the gloom of night. With the opening of a new school term the lamp of learning has been rekindled to do away with ignorance, or *mental* darkness. The lamp of all pure arts and useful knowledge needs to burn brightly in our world.

There is yet another kind of darkness. This is *spiritual* darkness—the gloom of unbelief, separation from God, hopelessness. Christian education on all levels seeks to lead learners to Jesus Christ, the Light of the world.

The means used for spiritual enlightenment is the Word of God. The psalmist declares (119:105): "Thy Word is a lamp to my feet and a light to my path." The Gospel that shines brightly from the pages of Holy Scripture does more than teach us how to live in this world; it shows us the way to heaven through faith in Jesus Christ. "How precious is the book divine, By inspiration given! Bright as a lamp its teachings shine To guide our souls to heaven."

In the Old Testament God directed Moses: ". . . a lamp [shall] be set to burn continually." The burning lamp in the tabernacle symbolized the continual presence of God with His people. The ever-burning light in some churches today reminds us that Christ is present in the Word and sacraments. It signifies that Christians, gathered about the Word, worship God at all times and places. "O Word of God incarnate, O Wisdom from on high, O Truth unchanged, unchanging, O Light of our dark sky: We praise you for the radiance That from the hallowed page, A lantern to our footsteps, Shines on from age to age."

The Church—
Like Noah's Ark

From most ancient times the church has been compared to a ship. An old document, *Apostolic Constitutions,* dating back to about the third century, gives this instruction on how to build a church: "Let the building be oblong, toward the east, like a ship." To this day we refer to the main part of the church as the nave, from the Latin *navis,* a ship.

As the ship sails through troubled seas, so the church, amid the waves and winds of adversity, is on its heavenward voyage. Jesus Christ, the captain of our salvation (Hebrews 2:10 KJV), is in charge. The passengers are the church members, served by a crew of pastors, teachers, counselors, and others who minister.

A bit more Biblical, as a symbol of the church, is Noah's ark. During the great Flood the ark (like the church, as it appears to the onlooker, hardly a graceful vessel) kept eight souls from perishing. These were Noah, his wife, his sons Shem, Ham, and Japheth, and their wives.

In his First Epistle St. Peter draws a parallel between two kinds of water. He recalls that these eight persons were not only saved *from* the Flood water but also *by* it, for it bore up the ark in which Noah and his family found a sanctuary. Then he speaks of the water whereby the church saves people: "Baptism, which corresponds to this, now saves you" (3:21). The church, as a New Testament Noah's ark, is equipped with the means of salvation: Word and sacraments.

In a Reformation hymn we speak thus to God: "See round your ark the hungry billows curling, See how your foes their banners are unfurling. Lord, while their poisoned arrows they are hurling, You can preserve us."

The Olive Branch: Hope and Peace

Olive trees were extensively cultivated in the Holy Land. They are frequently mentioned in the Bible. Olive trees grew in the Garden of Gethsemane; the name means "oil press." Olive oil had many uses: as food, for anointing the body, and as medicine. With olive oil kings were anointed.

The prophet Hosea declares (14:6): "[Israel's] shoots shall spread out; his beauty shall be like the olive." This imagery may have prompted St. Paul to compare spiritual Israel to an olive tree into which the Gentiles, as branches of a wild olive, were grafted. The olive tree is a picture of the Christian church.

The olive branch as a symbol of victory, hope, and expectation of new life dates back to the time when the waters of the Deluge were abating. We are told that Noah sent out a dove from the ark. Then we read: "The dove came back to him . . . and lo, in her mouth a freshly plucked olive leaf; so Noah knew that the waters had subsided . . . ." With this sign of hope, the human race could make its second start.

The olive branch is best known as a symbol of peace. Olive oil, as a home remedy, was able to soothe pain. Thus in Christian symbolism the olive sprig points to the grace of Jesus Christ which gives peace to troubled souls.

In secular usage the olive branch represents an overture for peace. *Roget's Thesaurus* lists "olive branch" with such synonymns as "peace offering, preliminaries of peace, truce, armistice." Perhaps the connection is that cultivation of the olive is a peaceful pursuit, much harmed by war. At any rate, readiness to forgive and to make peace is a Christian virtue, stemming from the peace we have with God in Christ Jesus.

The Open Bible

There are several symbols for the Bible, including that of a burning lamp. This image is based on Psalm 119:105: "Thy Word is a lamp to my feet and a light to my path." The Bible has opened many hearts and minds for serving Jesus Christ, the Light of the world.

Another, very obvious, symbol for the Holy Scripture is the open book. "Scripture" means something written, from the Latin *scribere,* to write. The Greek New Testament uses both the singular and the plural: *graphe* and *graphai*—Scripture and Scriptures—from *graphein,* to write. The word "Bible" comes from the Greek *biblion,* a little book.

Other names for the Bible are: Holy Writ, Sacred Writings (2 Timothy 3:15, Revised Standard Version), Book of Books. The Old Testament Scriptures are often referred to as the Law and the Prophets, and the full Bible as the writings of the prophets and apostles. The Bible makes known God's will and His love in Jesus Christ. This is the Law and the Gospel.

The symbol of the *open* Bible is significant. Time was when the Bible, written in languages the average person could not understand, was a closed book. Thanks to the work of Bible translators, among whom Martin Luther and William Tyndale stand tall, God's Word is widely accessible. In our day many new versions and paraphrases have further opened God's Book. Many Bible translators are now going out to remote parts of the world. They put unwritten languages into writing and then translate the Bible into those languages.

May we always honor what England's great prime minister, William E. Gladstone, called "the impregnable rock of Holy Scripture."

St. Michael and All Angels

Sept. 29 is set aside on the church calendar as the Day of St. Michael and All Angels.

St. Michael is pictured in Christian art as a militant archangel clad in full armor and wielding a flaming sword. His shield has a cross with rounded corners. His great opponent was Satan, against whom he waged war in heaven, as we read in Revelation 12:7-8: "Now war arose in heaven, Michael and his angels fighting against the dragon; and the dragon and his angels fought, but they were defeated and there was no longer any place for them in heaven." The poet John Milton dwells at length on this subject in *Paradise Lost.*

St. Michael is sometimes pictured as bearing a scroll on which these words are written: *Quis est Deus?* This question reflects the meaning of his name: "Who is like God?"

The Letter of Jude cites St. Michael as chivalrous and forebearing. When contending with the devil over the body of Moses, he did not revile his opponent but commended the matter to God, saying: "The Lord rebuke you." In this respect he is to be an example to Christians.

St. Michael has been regarded as the guardian angel of the church, who opposes the enemies of God and of God's people. The church is mindful not only of high-ranking angels such as Michael and Gabriel, but also of the other angels who continually praise God, carry out His commands, and serve people. In the Holy Communion liturgy the congregation sings: "With angels and archangels and with all the company of heaven we laud and magnify your glorious name, evermore praising you . . ." As Christians we praise God with and for His angels.

The Office of the Keys

Keys have significance in the Bible. Isaiah (22:22) mentions "the key of the house of David," that is, the church. In the Book of Revelation (3:7) the exalted Christ claims the power of this key for Himself. He it is "who opens and no one shall shut, who shuts and no one opens." Whoever has the key controls the house. Our Lord is in charge of His church. He has the power to forgive and retain sins, thus opening and shutting heaven.

The power of the keys that He possesses Christ entrusts to His church. The Office of the Keys is "the peculiar church power which Christ has given to His church on earth." ("Peculiar" here means that the power has been committed distinctively and exclusively to the church.) It is the power "to forgive the sins of penitent sinners, but to retain the sins of the impenitent as long as they do not repent."

When the church pronounces Christ's forgiveness, it uses the absolving key; when it excommunicates, it uses the binding key. These two aspects of the Office of the Keys are represented by the two keys crossed like the letter X.

The crossed keys in some instances refer to St. Peter, to whom Jesus said: "I will give you the keys of the kingdom of heaven, and whatever you bind on earth shall be bound in heaven, and whatever you loose on earth shall be loosed in heaven" (Matthew 16:19). In a later passage (Matthew 18:18) Jesus addresses these words to all the disciples, and He makes plain that the Office of the Keys is given to the church. Likewise in John 20:23 it is reported that Jesus breathed on His disciples, telling them: "If you forgive the sins of any, they are forgiven; if you retain the sins of any, they are retained."

The Sacrament of Holy Baptism

From ancient times various symbols have been used in Christian art for Holy Baptism. Among them are: the escallop shell with three drops of water to designate the Triune God into whose name the person is baptized; the eight-pointed star of baptismal regeneration; two stags drinking water; the rock from which living water flows.

The universal symbol of Holy Baptism is the font. It is shaped as either round or as eight-sided. In Christian symbolism, for reasons unknown, the number eight represents the new birth in Christ. The cover of the font tapers off into a cross, to symbolize that Christ's merit, earned on the cross, is imparted to the individual baptized. Also the dove is at times seen on the font cover, reminding us that in this sacrament the Holy Spirit creates and strengthens faith.

In times past the baptismal font was often located at the church entrance, as if to say that it is through Holy Baptism that we enter the holy Christian church, the communion of saints. Nowadays the font is placed toward the front of the church so that the congregation can better participate in this sacred act.

Holy Baptism is a sacrament, a means of grace. It was instituted by Christ when He declared: "Make disciples of all nations, baptizing them in the name of the Father and of the Son and of the Holy Spirit." The rite of baptism signifies our burial and resurrection with Christ, as St. Paul teaches in Romans chapter 6. But it not only signifies but also effects the death to sin and the daily rising to newness of life. St. Peter told the Pentecost audience: "Be baptized ... in the name of Jesus Christ for the remission of sins."

The Sacrament of Holy Communion

The sacrament that Christ instituted on the evening before His death is His last will and testament, to be observed unchanged until He comes again on the Last Day. It goes by various names: Holy Communion, the Lord's Supper, the Lord's Table, Holy Eucharist, the Breaking of Bread.

Christian symbolism has portrayed this sacrament in various ways: as chalice and ciborium (containers for wine and wafers), or as a chalice with the host rising out of it. Shown here is the dual symbol of wheat and grapes, the products from which the visible elements are derived: bread prepared from flour, and wine, the fruit of the vine.

Along with Holy Baptism, Holy Communion is a sacrament, that is, a sacred act, ordained by Christ, in which He by certain external means, connected with His Word, offers, conveys, and seals to Christians the grace which Christ has merited. In Holy Communion the consecrated bread and wine, received in a natural way, convey Christ's true body and blood in a supernatural manner. We call it a sacramental eating and drinking.

The Bible declares that there is koinonia (communion, fellowship, togetherness) between the blessed bread and wine and Christ's true body and blood, respectively. The elements remain bread and wine, but in the sacrament, that is, in the eating and drinking of them in Holy Communion, Christ's true body and blood are received. The doctrine involved here is that of the Real Presence. All who commune receive the Lord's body and blood, the unbelievers (should there be such at the Lord's table) for judgment, but believers for the strengthening of faith in the forgiveness of sins and for growth in holy living.

Martin Luther's Coat of Arms

The beginning of the reform of the church is dated Oct. 31, 1517, the eve of All Saints' Day, when Martin Luther posted his *Ninety-Five Theses* on a church door in Wittenberg, Germany. In commemoration of that event the Lutheran Church, as well as all Protestantism, observes the Festival of the Reformation.

Martin Luther's coat of arms is a suitable symbol for the Reformation. It shows the cross on a heart, imposed on the Messianic rose and surrounded by a circle to denote eternity.

The meaning of the cross is evident. Luther said: "... in my heart [is] the image of a Man hanging on a cross." To Luther—and to all Christians with him—the Messianic rose has this significance: "The Christian's heart is resting on roses E'en while beneath the cross it reposes." The circle refers to the permanence of God's Word, as stated in Latin: *Verbum Dei manet in aeternum.* The words are those of St. Peter, quoting Isaiah: "The Word of the Lord abides forever."

Originally Luther did not have churchwide reform in mind. His intent in 1517 was to offer 95 propositions for debate concerning church abuses, particularly the sale of indulgences. He wanted to probe into the whole penance system, since He believed the penitent sinner is declared just by faith in Christ.

Another symbol suitable for Reformation Day is the lamp, which stands for the knowledge of God's Word. God used Luther as a lamplighter. His translation of the Bible, completed in 1534, enabled the people to read the Word of God in their own language. Luther's writing and preaching enabled the Gospel to shine brightly again in all the world.

All Saints— God's Harvest

All Saints' Day was observed already at an early date in the church's history. Its intent was to honor the memory of departed Christians, particularly martyrs. In about the middle of the ninth century that day was shifted from May 13 to Nov. 1. All Saints' Day was retained in the church of the Reformation, although the later emphasis on Reformation Day, observed the day before, has taken some attention away from it.

In most of the symbols for the saints the crown is in evidence. The crown of life is given to all who persevere in the faith. In the Book of Revelation the Lord promises (2:10): "Be faithful unto death, and I will give you the crown of life."

The symbol shown here has the crown holding the good wheat—the faithful whom the Lord of the church has gathered for His harvest. In the parable of the wheat and tares Jesus declares: "At harvest time I will tell the reapers . . . gather the wheat into My barn" (Matthew 13:30). Their souls are already garnered.

The symbol further shows the Alpha and Omega, and the Chi Rho, which are designations for the Savior, who has made the harvest of souls possible.

The place where a granary stood in old Boston is now the site of a cemetery where Paul Revere, John Hancock, and other patriots rest. It is called "Old Granary Cemetery," a fitting name in view of the Lord's harvest of souls.

This familiar hymn sounds the right keynote for the observance of the day: "For all the saints who from their labors rest, All who by faith before the world confessed Your name, O Jesus, be forever blest. Alleluia! Alleluia!

The Rite of Confirmation

Confirmation is a church rite not specifically commanded in the Bible, although St. Paul does commend Timothy for making "the good confession in the presence of many witnesses." Confirmation in part involves the confession of faith.

Specifically, confirmation is the reaffirmation of the baptismal vow. The confirmand, having previously been baptized, now renews and confirms faith in the Triune God. At baptism the sponsors spoke for the child. At confirmation the catechumens, after due instruction in the Word of God, confess their faith with their own mouths. They, so to speak, take their baptismal covenant upon themselves, as persons who have reached the age of discretion.

The confirmands have previously been examined and have rendered an account of their faith. They are now regarded as young adults and are received into full communicant membership, with all rights and privileges, particularly the reception of Holy Communion.

The symbol shown above is self-explanatory. Another symbol for confirmation shows Christ on a shield surmounted by the figure of the Holy Spirit, descending and sending forth rays of light to denote spiritual enlightenment. This symbol is in keeping with the blessing spoken with the laying on of hands: "God, the Father of our Lord Jesus Christ, give you His Holy Spirit, the Spirit of wisdom and knowledge, of grace and prayer, of power and strength, of sanctification and the fear of God." The confirmand's prayer is: "My God, accept my heart this day And make it always Thine That I from Thee no more may stray, No more from Thee decline."

The Sign of Holy Matrimony

Marriage is of utmost significance to Christians. This sacred rite and estate can be symbolized by two clasped hands, in agreement with the line in the wedding service: "Join your right hands." Sometimes a third hand enters the scene—the hand of God extended in benediction.

A more elaborate symbol of holy matrimony consists of the cross, interlocking wedding rings, and lit candles. The cross stands for Christ, who is always to be kept in the picture, for He blesses the marriage. The rings are emblems of the troth both bridegroom and bride have plighted. Without beginning and without end, they signify the promise of faithfulness until death itself severs the marriage bond. The burning candles indicate the light of God's Word, which is to shine in the new home.

Holy matrimony was instituted by God Himself in the Garden of Eden. Because it is God's own ordinance, it is honorable in all and should be kept in honor by all. The Lord Jesus honored this estate by His presence at the marriage at Cana and by performing the first of His miracles there to help the bridal couple (John 2:1-11). St. Paul, speaking of the mystic union between Christ and His church, holds it up as an example of the love that should rule the marriage relationship (Ephesians 5:25-33).

The church prays for those who enter marriage: "O perfect Love, all human thought transcending, Lowly we kneel in prayer before Thy throne That theirs may be the love which knows no ending, Whom Thou forevermore dost join in one."

 # Jesus Christ, Alpha and Omega

When we come to the end of the church year and look ahead to the beginning of another, it is good to look to Jesus, the Author and Finisher of our faith (Hebrews 12:2 KJV). He is "the Alpha and the Omega, the First and the Last, the Beginning and the End" (Revelation 22:13). He who speaks these words in the Book of Revelation is our exalted Savior Jesus Christ. Alpha and Omega are the first and last letters of the Greek alphabet. The Son of God is from first to last, from eternity to eternity, "the same yesterday and today and forever."

The Alpha and Omega monogram will more readily remind us of the Savior when other symbols of Christ are used with it. In the symbol shown above, derived from one found in an ancient catacomb, the Alpha and Omega are combined with the Christogram, Chi Rho.

While the Alpha and Omega monogram asserts the eternity of Jesus Christ, it has a message for the Advent season ahead. The great truth is that the eternal Son of God entered time and space and became a human being. An ancient hymn refers to this mystery of the Incarnation: "Of the Father's love begotten Ere the words began to be, He is Alpha and Omega, He the Source, the Ending He. . . ."

Jesus Christ is the beginning and end of our faith. As the church concludes another year of grace, it is good to remember that our Lord Jesus is eternal, unchangeable. What is more, He is merciful, loving, faithful, as He asserts in His "I am" statements: I am the Good Shepherd, the Door, the Way, the Truth, the Life. To Him be all glory!